How Do They Grow?

From Chick to Chicken

by Jillian Powell

RAINTREE
STECK-VAUGHN
RSVP PUBLISHERS

A Harcourt Company

Austin   New York
www.raintreesteckvaughn.com

WILMETTE PUBLIC LIBRARY

Published by Raintree Steck-Vaughn Publishers,
an imprint of Steck-Vaughn Company

Library of Congress Cataloging-in-Publication Data

Powell, Jillian.
   From chick to chicken / Jillian Powell.
      p. cm.-- (How do they grow)
   Includes bibliographical references (p.).
   ISBN 0-7398-4427-X
      1. Chicks--Juvenile literature. 2. Chickens--Development--Juvenile literature. [1. Chickens. 2. Animals--Infancy.] I. Title.

SF498.4 .P69 2001
636.5'07--dc21   2001019199

Printed in Italy. Bound in the United States.
1 2 3 4 5 6 7 8 9 0 LB 05 04 03 02 01

Picture acknowledgments

Agripicture (Peter Dean) 12, 13, 14, 15, 28, 29; FLPA 4 (W. Adams/Sunset), 10 (Derek Middleton), 20 (John Watkins), 21 (John Watkins), 26 (Gerard Laci); Holt Studios International 16 (Inga Spence) 17 (Nigel Cattlin); 24 (Inga Spence); HWPL 18, 25; NHPA 6 (David Woodfall), 8 (E. A Janes), 9 (E. A Janes); RSPCA Photolibrary title page (Jeff du Fea), 5 (E. A Janes), 11 (E. A Janes), 19 (Colin Seddon), 22 (Angela Hampton), 23 (Andrew Linscott), 27 (E. A Janes); Science Photo Library 7 (Hugh Turvey).

Contents

Words in **bold** in the text can be found in the glossary on page 30.

From Egg to Chick

This **hen** has laid some eggs.
She has made a nest of straw.
She sits on the eggs to keep them
safe and warm until they **hatch**.

On this farm, the hens are kept with **roosters**. Hens **mate** with the **roosters**. Then baby chicks can grow inside the eggs that the hens lay.

Inside the Eggs

A hen lays an egg almost every day.
Each egg rolls into her nest. The eggshells are
strong so the chicks can grow safely inside them.

Inside each egg is a pocket of air so the chick can breathe. The yellow **yolk** is food for the baby bird as it grows.

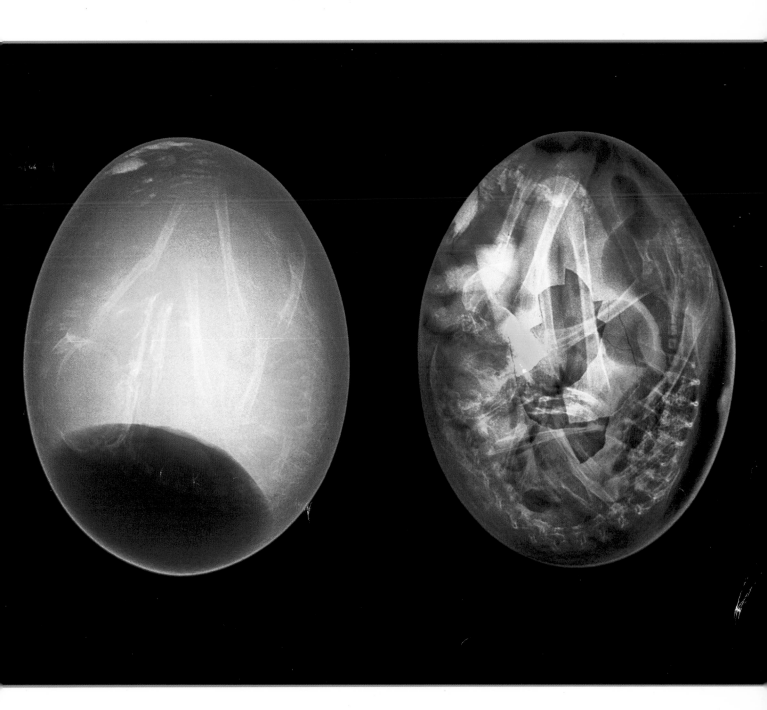

Ready to Hatch

After 21 days the baby chick is ready to hatch. It breaks its way out of the shell using a sharp point on its beak. This is called its egg tooth.

This chick has just hatched. Its wings are tiny, and its feet are big for its body. Its fine, soft feathers are wet at first. This **down** becomes dry and fluffy.

Young Chicks

The chicks stay close to their mother.
She keeps them safe and warm. They will
follow her everywhere.

These chicks are just a day old. Their soft down is yellow and fluffy. When they are older, they will grow feathers like their mother's.

At the Hatchery

On big farms, chicks are hatched from eggs in a **hatchery**. The eggs are kept in trays that keep them safe and warm, just like a mother hen does.

The eggs are turned several times a day, just like a hen turns the eggs in her nest. Twenty-one days after the eggs have been laid they hatch into chicks.

13

Hatchery Chicks

In a hatchery, lots of chicks hatch together. These chicks often go to **broiler farms**. On a broiler farm chicks will grow until they are big enough to give us chicken meat.

Females can be chosen from a batch of chicks. These females go to egg farms where hens lay eggs for people to eat.

At the Broiler Farm

A farm worker is placing these chicks in the broiler shed. They will spend their lives in this shed, where they will grow quickly.

These chicks are now seven days old. They have plenty of food and water to drink. The chicks are feeding on food made from **grains** that helps them to grow.

Chickens for Meat

These chicks are a few weeks old. As they get bigger, feathers replace their soft yellow down. When they are five to eight weeks old, they will be big enough to sell for meat.

These broiler chickens are kept on a **free-range farm**. This means they spend part of their lives outdoors. So they can scratch around outside to find food. The chickens are now fully grown.

The Egg Farm

On an egg farm, the farmer keeps female chicks. These chicks will grow into hens that lay eggs for people to eat. The lamp is keeping the chicks warm.

These young hens are six weeks old. They hatched in the spring. They will be ready to start laying their own eggs in the autumn.

21

Free-Range Hens

This hen is 20 weeks old. Her wings and feathers are now fully grown. She is ready to lay her own eggs. These eggs will be sold for people to eat.

Hens kept on free-range egg farms can go outdoors in the daytime. They sleep in the hen house at night to keep them safe from foxes.

Laying Eggs to Eat

Hens kept on free-range farms lay their eggs
in a box like this. The box is in a hen house.
This means the hen and her eggs are safe
and warm in the straw nest.

This farm worker gathers free-range eggs.

The eggs roll out of the box.

The worker puts them into trays.

The Breeding Farm

Some female chicks grow into hens that are
kept for **breeding**. They live in breeding coops
and eat plenty of grain to help them
lay lots of eggs.

The farmer keeps roosters to mate with the hens. When they have mated, baby chicks start to grow inside the eggs that the hens lay.

Eggs for Hatching

First the hens lay their eggs. Then the eggs are
collected from the boxes at the breeding house.
The best eggs go to the hatchery and
are kept warm in trays.

This chick has just hatched from an egg at
the hatchery. Hens can lay eggs every day.
So chicks are hatched all through the year.

Glossary

Breeding When a male and female produce young.

Broiler farm (BROY-lur) A farm which produces chickens for meat. They are called broilers.

Down (doun) The fine, soft feathers of a young bird.

Free-range farm (free-ranje) A farm that allows its chickens or hens to go outdoors in the daytime.

Grains (graynz) The seeds of cereal crops like wheat and maize.

Hatch (hach) When a baby bird breaks out of its eggshell.

Hatchery (HACH-er-ee) A place where eggs are kept warm in trays before the chicks hatch.

Hen A female chicken.

Mate When a male and female come together to have babies.

Roosters (ROO-sturz) Male chickens.

Yolk (yoke) The yellow part of the inside of an egg. It is food for a growing chick.

Further Information

Books

Back, Christine. *Chicken and Egg.* (Stopwatch series). Silver Burdett Press, 1991.

Burroughs, Nigel. *Nature's Chicken: The Story of Today's Chicken Farms.* Book Publishers Co., 1992.

Hansel, Ann L. *Chickens.* (Farm Animals series). ABDO Publishers Co., 1998.

Potter, Tessa. *Hens.* (Animal World Series). Raintree Steck-Vaughn, 1990.

Royston, Angela. *Life Cycle of a Chicken.* Heinemann Library, 1998.

Stone, Lynn M. *Chickens.* (Farm Animals Discovery Library). Rourke Corporation, 1990.

Wallace, Karen. *My Hen Is Dancing.* (Read and Wonder Books). Candlewick Press, 1994.

Video

Farm Animals narrated by Johnny Morris (Dorling Kindersley)

On the Farm: Baby Animals (Dorling Kindersley)

Lets Go to the Farm/Baby Animals (Countryside Products). Visit their website at: **www.countrysidevideos.com**

Websites

www.aeb.org

The American egg board site has all sorts of information about eggs and poultry, with egg facts and an "eggcylopaedia."

www.ansi.okstate.edu/poultry/

The Oklahoma State University Department of Animal Science. Learn all about different breeds of chickens, geese, ducks, and other poultry.

www.kiddyhouse.com/farm/chicken

A fun site about chickens for kids and teachers. Stories, facts, and games.

Useful addresses

National 4-H Council
7100 CT Avenue
Chevy Chase, MD 20815
Phone: (301) 961-2800

Index

B
beak 8
breathing 7
breeding coops 26
broiler farm 14, 16

C
chicks 5, 6, 7, 8, 9,
  10, 11, 12, 13, 14,
  15, 16, 17, 18, 20,
  26, 27, 29
down 9, 11, 18

E
egg farms 15, 20-21
egg tooth 8
eggs 4, 5, 6, 7, 12, 13,
  15, 20, 21, 22, 24,
  25, 26, 27, 28, 29

F
feathers 9, 11, 18, 22
food 7, 17, 19
foxes 23
free-range farms 19,
  23-25

H
hatchery 12, 14, 28,
  29
hatching 4, 8, 9, 12,
  13, 14, 29

M
mating 5, 27
meat 14, 18

N
nest 4, 6, 13, 24

R
roosters 5, 27

W
water 17
wings 9, 22

Y
yolk 7